IMAGES OF
HUDDERSFIELD
RUGBY LEAGUE FOOTBALL CLUB

IMAGES OF
HUDDERSFIELD
RUGBY LEAGUE FOOTBALL CLUB

DAVID GRONOW

The
History
Press

For Madeleine, Jonathan and Sarah,
Ben, Kate and Rebecca

Frontispiece: Frank 'Spanky' Dyson was a solid, reliable full-back who established new Huddersfield records in goal-kicking between 1949 and 1963 which will take some surpassing. In making 367 appearances, his Huddersfield club record of goals in a career (958) and points in a career (2,072) still remain intact.

First published 2010

The History Press
The Mill, Brimscombe Port
Stroud, Gloucestershire, GL5 2QG
www.thehistorypress.co.uk

British Library Cataloguing in Publication Data.
A catalogue record for this book is available from the British
Library.

ISBN 978 0 7524 5135 0

Typesetting and origination by The History Press
Printed in Great Britain

CONTENTS

Chris Thorman has been a prolific scorer in Huddersfield Giants' Super League era. In two spells with the club he amassed 1,092 points comprising 75 tries, 393 goals and 6 drop goals in 165 (+11 sub) games. Here, Wakefield Trinity Wildcats' Sam Obst attempts to charge down Thorman's kick during the 2007 'Millenium Magic' weekend at Cardiff.

INTRODUCTION

At every club there's someone who can recite the names of the best-ever team and Huddersfield are no exception: Hunter, Henderson, Pepperell, Devery, Cooper, Ramsden, Banks, etc. That's a marvellous tribute, but those very players would be the first to acknowledge that it takes hundreds of players to contribute to a club's history.

The earliest record of a football match being played in the Huddersfield area is in 1848, when a team from Hepworth took on a team from Holmfirth near Whinney Bank in Holmfirth. Hepworth won a close-fought game which 'exhibited the usual amount of confusions and bloody noses.'

Huddersfield's history as a rugby club began as Huddersfield Athletic Club in 1864, one of the longest and most interesting in Yorkshire. Their first games were played at the Rifle Field, Trinity Street, before amalgamation in 1875 with St John's Cricket Club in the Fartown district, the two clubs agreeing a merger to form Huddersfield Cricket & Athletic Club (HC & AC). The first game of rugby at Fartown was on 2 November 1878 when Huddersfield entertained Manchester Rangers. Huddersfield's links with rugby league became enshrined in folklore after the historic meeting at The George Hotel in the town on 29 August 1895, when the decision was taken to form a Northern Rugby Football Union and split from the governing body.

Huddersfield enjoyed a glorious era in the years leading up to the First World War – known as the 'Team of All Talents' – in 1914/15, sweeping all before them and becoming the second team to win 'All Four Cups'. The inter-war years were equally as glorious as the past and was a golden age for the club. However, while trophies would be collected post-war until the mid-1960s, Huddersfield would never return to the heights of that magical period. It seems that for every success the club has enjoyed, it has also endured long and sometimes traumatic periods of failure.

By the 1980s and '90s, the Fartown ground had fallen into disrepair and the club were regularly finishing in the lower reaches of the league. However, in 1992 the unthinkable happened: Huddersfield played their last match at Fartown. They then moved in with Huddersfield Town AFC at Leeds Road, before taking a share in the McAlpine (now the Galpharm) Stadium in 1994 and subsequently gaining admittance to the Super League in 1998. The Giants went from strength to strength under the guidance of chairman Ken Davy, reaching the final of the Powergen Challenge Cup in 2006, also achieving a Super League play-off place for the first time in 2007. Under Australian coach Nathan Brown, 2009 was undoubtedly a season of outstanding achievement for Huddersfield – the Giants reached the Carnegie Challenge Cup Final at Wembley and the end-of-season play-offs after finishing an all-time high third position in Super League XIV as well as being chosen as engage Super League Club of the Year.

It is hoped that this book will evoke many memories and triumphs of years gone by, as well as provide a look at this great club since its return to the top echelon of British rugby league.

David Gronow, 2010

ACKNOWLEDGEMENTS

Obtaining the material in this book has involved a great deal of assistance from others who have been generous in providing pictures and information. I must thank Bradford Museums/Galleries and Heritage, Sig Kasatkin and Dave Williams (www.rlphotos.com), the Stephen Lockwood Collection, the World Rugby Museum (Twickenham) and Robert Gate – an unlimited source of rugby league knowledge.

I am also indebted to the *Huddersfield Examiner* and John Rushworth (www.photoeye. co.uk), the Huddersfield Giants' official club photographer, for allowing me to use images from their collections. Many of the photographs in this book are from my private collection, if copyrights have been infringed, then it is without intent.

I must also acknowledge specific cross-reference to *Claret and Gold 1895–1946* by Stanley Chadwick, the Fartown Yearbooks compiled by A.N. Gaulton and Peter Crabtree, plus statistics and text from *Football: The Rugby Union Game* published in 1892 and edited by the Revd F. Marshall.

ONE

IN THE BEGINNING:
1864 TO 1895

The gymnasium in St John's Road was headquarters of Huddersfield Cricket & Athletic Club until the summer of 1906. Formed as Huddersfield Athletic Club in 1864, amalgamation with St John's Cricket Club took place on 27 November 1875, with the first football match played at Fartown on 2 November 1878 against Manchester Rangers.

Two football cards of Huddersfield from the 1880s depicting the club colours of Claret and Gold. In the last two decades of the nineteenth century an entrepreneurial Yorkshireman, John Baines of Manningham, began to produce packets of football cards which sold at six for a halfpenny.

The Huth brothers. *From left to right:* Frank, Harry and Fred. Harry Huth was the first member of the Huddersfield club to play for England. He and his two brothers, Fred and Frank, all played for Yorkshire, appearing in the same team against Cheshire in 1878.

The England team who played Scotland in Edinburgh on 10 March 1879. *Back row, left to right:* H. Huth (Huddersfield), R. Walker (Manchester), L. Stokes (Blackheath), F.R. Adams (Richmond), S. Neame (Old Cheltonians), G. Harrison (Hull), N.F. McLeod (R.I.E. College), H.C. Rowley (Manchester), H.H. Taylor (St George's Hospital). *Middle row:* W.J. Penny (United Hospitals/Kings College Hospital), A. Budd (Blackheath), G.W. Burton (Blackheath), H.H. Springman (Liverpool), F.D. Fowler (Manchester). *Front row:* W.A.D. Evanson (Richmond), G.F. Vernon (Blackheath) reserve.

Ernest Woodhead was a tall, clever forward who played against Ireland in Dublin on 2 February 1880. At Edinburgh University he played as a three-quarter, but was subsequently a forward. He shone particularly in loose play and was a dangerous runner when in possession of the ball.

The Huddersfield team of 1881/2. *Back row, left to right:* J.J. Booth (Hon Sec), F.W. Walker, J. Clifford, George Crosland, Fred Huth, H. Huth (capt), B. Schofield, G.W. Bottomley, J.C. Wheatley, F.H. Walker (umpire). *Front row:* A.C. Sharpe, E.W.H. Anderson, H.B. Wilson, H.E. Calvert, L. Littlewood, J. Haigh, P.F. Holmes.

Huddersfield enjoyed the distinction of winning the Yorkshire Challenge Cup ('t'owd Tin Pot'), beating Wakefield Trinity by one goal to nothing at Halifax in 5 April 1890. *Back row, left to right:* J. Dyson, G. Harrop (Hon Sec), W.H. Eagland, L. Littlewood (umpire), F.W. Richmond, J.H. Shaw, W. Hirst (Hon Sec of HC & AC), J.W. Thewlis, T.H. Eagland, J.P. Crosland (president). *Middle row:* G. Mitchell, P. Jackson, H. Archer (capt), O. France, J. Schofield. *Front row:* J. Kaye, F. Walker, W. Lorriman, A.L. Brooke.

Jack Dyson, who played in Huddersfield's Yorkshire Challenge Cup-winning side of 1890, was the most dangerous scoring three-quarter of his day. A Yorkshire County player on numerous occasions, he was an exceedingly fast and strong runner. He gained his first international cap, scoring a try, as England beat Scotland by one goal and one try to nil in Edinburgh on 1 March 1890. He made a further appearance for England against Scotland, again in Edinburgh, on 5 March 1892.

There was general acknowledgement that the rugby teams of Yorkshire and Lancashire were the strongest in England and had been since the 1870s. This was the scene at Fartown, Huddersfield, on 28 November 1891 when a crowd of 23,270 watched the Roses match in atrocious weather. Dyson and Paisley of Huddersfield were in the Yorkshire side of which W.H. Bromet of Tadcaster was the captain.

A line-out is contested in the derby game between Huddersfield and Halifax (in hooped shirts) at Fartown in 1892. The line-out was a feature of the Northern Union until it was abolished in 1897.

The Huddersfield team of 1891.
Top row, left to right: G. Harrop,
W. Schofield, G. Mitchell,
W.H. Eagland, J. Kaye, D. Haigh,
R.F. Senior. *Middle row:* J. Dyson,
H. Archer (capt), A.L. Brooke.
Bottom: J.W. Thewlis, F. Walker,
F.W. Richmond, T.H. Eagland,
E.H. Shaw, P. Jackson.

Harry Lodge played for Huddersfield
from 1890 to 1896 and was captain
of the Fartowners during their
first season under the Northern
Union code. He played for Yorkshire
against Cumberland and Cheshire
in 1890/1, and against Somerset,
Devonshire and the Rest of England
in the 1892/3 season. He served
for twenty-one years on the
Huddersfield Football Committee,
including a year as chairman.

The Revd Francis Marshall was the self-appointed scourge of professionalism in the years before the Northern Union breakaway from the Rugby Football Union in 1895. A referee and Huddersfield committeeman until he resigned, he was more representative of the southern view than he was of the general opinion of the north.

A cartoon lampooning the divide in rugby featuring the Revd Francis Marshall, an arch-opponent of broken time payments, and James Miller, member for North Leeds on the Yorkshire committee. The caption underneath reads, 'Marshall: "Oh, fie, go away naughty boy. I don't play with boys who can't afford to take a holiday for football any day they like!" Miller: "Yes, that's just you to a T; you'd make it so that no lad whose father wasn't a millionaire could play at all in a really good team. For my part I see no reason why the men who make the money shouldn't have a share in the spending of it."'

TWO

THE
NORTHERN UNION ERA:
'TEAM OF ALL TALENTS'

The George Hotel, Huddersfield, at the turn of the twentieth century. It was here on 29 August 1895, in defiance of the English Rugby Football Union, that the historic meeting of twenty-one delegates from Yorkshire and Lancashire clubs adopted a resolution, 'that the clubs here represented decide to form a Northern Rugby Football Union, and pledge themselves to push forward without delay its establishment on the principle of payment of bona fide broken time only.'

John Clifford was the Huddersfield representative at the George Hotel meeting. A former captain of Huddersfield in the 1880s, Clifford rose to prominence in the Northern Union, being elected president in 1902 and acting as joint-manager with Joe Houghton (St Helens) of the first two touring teams to Australasia in 1910 and 1914.

Milford Sutcliffe played in Huddersfield's first Northern Union game against Wakefield Trinity at Fartown on 14 September 1895. He was the only Huddersfield player to represent Yorkshire in 1894/5. Sutcliffe played ten times for Yorkshire at league level between 1895 and 1899. He played 285 times for Huddersfield, scored 75 tries and kicked 18 goals. His playing career over, he was elected to the Huddersfield Football Committee and was subsequently a vice-president and life member of the club.

Huddersfield's first season in the Northern Union was one of 'disappointment and disaster' – only 10 games were won out of 42 played. A. Boothroyd headed the list of try-scorers with 18. This is the Huddersfield side in 1896. *Back row, left to right:* W. Stubbings, A. Boothroyd, J. Conley, J. Moxon, M. Sutcliffe (capt), T.E. Dickinson, T. Dickinson, J. Debney, A. Bennett. *Middle row:* H. Taylor, H.H. Wood, F. Bath, P.M. France, J.W. Bradley, A. Wilson, J. Clifford. *Front row:* W.H. Smith, F. Lorriman, J.F. Taylor.

Two players who played important roles in building up the team, which in later years was to make football history, joined the Huddersfield club in 1900. The first was William Farrington (Billy) Kitchin, a Cumberland three-quarter, who made his debut at Hull KR on 1 September 1900. Other than 1903/4 and 1904/5 seasons, he played for Huddersfield for eleven years (266 appearances, 211 tries, 17 goals), appeared eleven times for Cumberland from 1902 to 1912 and won two England caps. Kitchin was captain of the first Huddersfield team to win a cup under NU rules – the Yorkshire Challenge Cup on 27 November 1909.

The second to join was Llewellyn Deere of Mountain Ash, another three-quarter back who played in the Huddersfield colours for the first time against Leeds Parish Church at Fartown on 20 October 1900. He played 173 times for Huddersfield (80 tries, 10 goals) and in later years assisted Merthyr Tydfil, the first Welsh club to embrace the NU game.

The Huddersfield team that played Hull at The Boulevard on 1 January 1903. *Back row, left to right:* Joe Clifford (chairman), F.H. Chambers, P. Driver, E. Knight, T. Dyson (reserve), A. Larard, M. Sutcliffe. *Middle row:* A. Hirst, W. Thomas, L. Deere (capt), H. Naylor, B. Furness, S. Pool. *Front row:* P. Holroyd, F. Dewhirst, F. Littlewood, W. Kitchin, A. Wimpenny.

The Huddersfield team of 1906/7. *Back row, left to right:* A. Bennett (trainer), W. Kitchin, W. Ainley, J. Barton, N. Micklethwaite, F. Balmforth, J. Cole, A. Swinden, H. Bennett (assistant trainer). *Front row:* P. Holroyd, E. Sykes, W. Patchett, J. Bartholomew, J. Jagger, H. Wagstaff. The 1906/7 season also heralded the debut of one of the most famous players ever to wear the Claret and Gold jersey, Harold Wagstaff, signed on 2 November 1906, aged 15 years 175 days old.

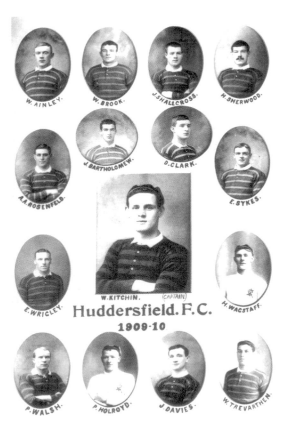

The 1909/10 season marked the beginning
of Huddersfield's cup-winning tradition. The
Fartowners won the Yorkshire Challenge Cup
beating Batley 21–0 at Headingley, Leeds, on
27 November 1909. Included in the side was
Australian Abe Rosenfeld, New Zealander
Edgar Wrigley, the first colonial player signed
by Huddersfield, and Douglas Clark from
Brookland Rovers in Cumberland.

All dressed up! The Yorkshire Cup was brought
home to Huddersfield and on arrival the team
was escorted by the Almondbury Brass Band
to the George Hotel. Afterwards the players
and officials toured the town in an illuminated
tram-car.

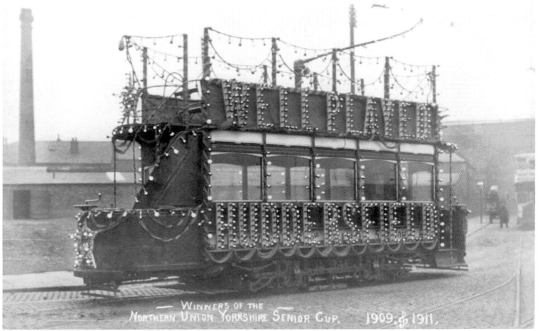

Edgar Wrigley, a New Zealand rugby union international, hailed from Masterton in the Wairarapa region of the country. Following his tour with the 1907/8 'All Golds', Wrigley signed for Huddersfield on 5 September 1908. He made 169 appearances for the Fartowners (84 tries, 162 goals).

Action from the game between Keighley and Huddersfield at Lawkholme Lane on 1 October 1910. Fartowners Percy Holroyd, Pat Walsh and John Shallcross await the outcome of the scrummage.

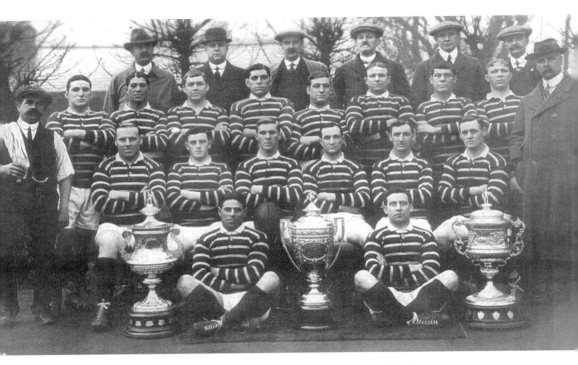

Following the 1909 Yorkshire Cup success, Huddersfield went on to dominate the sport. In 1911/12 they won the League Championship, Yorkshire Cup and Yorkshire League. *Back row, left to right:* John Clifford, R. Lockwood, Joe Clifford, H. Lodge, M. Sutcliffe, H. Bennett (assistant trainer). *Middle row:* A. Bennett (trainer), D. Clark, W. Trevarthen, J.W. Higson, B. Gronow, F. Longstaff, W. Brook, H. Sherwood, H. Walton, Chas Sykes. *Front row:* E. Wrigley, S. Moorhouse, H. Wagstaff (capt), J. Davies, T. Grey, W.F. Kitchin. *Seated on floor:* Yorkshire Cup, A. Rosenfeld, Yorkshire League Cup, M. Holland, Northern League Cup.

Fred Longstaff, a Bradfordian, made his debut for Huddersfield against Halifax at Fartown on 23 December 1911, and played 134 times (18 tries, 27 goals). He played for England in 1911/12, represented Yorkshire twice and was one of six Huddersfield players selected to tour Australia in 1914, playing in the first Test match at Sydney, where he kicked two goals in a 23–5 victory. Longstaff was killed in action at the Somme on 22 July 1916, at the early age of twenty-five years old.

Huddersfield 1912/13, winners of the Northern League Cup, Northern Challenge Cup and Yorkshire League Cup. *Back row, left to right:* T.H. Grey, M. Sutcliffe (committee), Joe Clifford (chairman). *Third row:* A. Bennett (trainer), A. Lee, John Clifford (vice-president), D. Clark, A. Swinden, E. Wrigley, F. Longstaff, J.W. Higson, J. Chilcott, B. Gronow, H. Bennett (assistant trainer). *Second row:* M. Holland, J. Davies, H. Wagstaff (capt), T. Gleeson, G. Todd, S. Moorhouse. *Front row:* Northern League Cup, A. Rosenfeld, Northern Challenge Cup, J. Rogers, Yorkshire League Cup.

Huddersfield 1913/14, winners of the Yorkshire Challenge Cup, Yorkshire League and Northern League Cup runners-up. *Back row, left to right:* G. Todd, J. Davies, M. Holland, T.H. Grey. *Middle row:* A. Rosenfeld, T. Gleeson, H. Wagstaff (capt), S. Moorhouse, B. Gronow. *Front row:* J.W. Higson, D. Clark, A. Lee, F. Longstaff, J. Chilcott, A. Swinden.

Albert Aaron Rosenfeld, the greatest try-scorer the Northern Union had produced – a perfect running machine at the end of an inspired back line, whose 80 tries in the 1913/14 season has never been matched. 'Rozzy' joined Huddersfield at the conclusion of the Australian Tour of 1908/9. He topped the rugby league try-scoring charts with totals of 40, 78, 56, 80 and 56 tries in five seasons from 1910 to 1915. He made 285 appearances for the Fartowners, scoring 366 tries and kicking 2 goals.

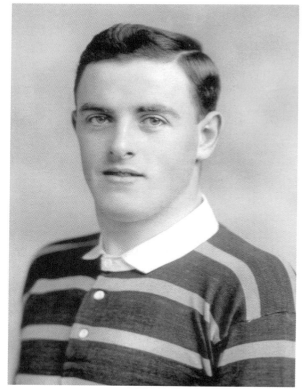

Stanley Moorhouse was a product of local schools football. He was a renowned winger for Huddersfield, Yorkshire and England in a glorious career between 1909 and 1922, when his partnership with Harold Wagstaff proved to be a deadly combination. Moorhouse played in 262 games for Huddersfield, scoring 251 tries, kicking 1 goal.

Harold Wagstaff, born at Underbank, Holmfirth, was 15 years 175 days old when he made his Huddersfield debut against Bramley on 10 November 1906. The career of the legendary Wagstaff, who was to be christened the 'Prince of Centres', had begun. During the nineteen years he was at Huddersfield he made 436 appearances (175 tries, 12 goals) and was captain of the Great Britain side that won the historic 'Rorkes Drift' Test in 1914.

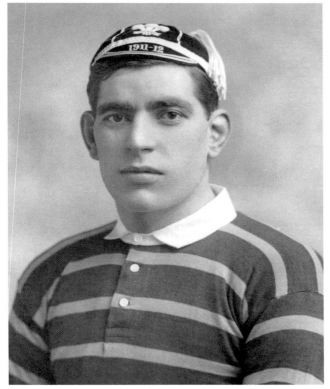

Ben Gronow joined Huddersfield from Bridgend RU, Wales, on 14 May 1910. He played 7 times for Great Britain and made two Lions Tours to Australia in 1920 and 1924. A prolific goal-kicker, his 147 goals in the 1919/20 season is to this day a Huddersfield club record of goals in a season. In a playing career for Huddersfield he made 395 appearances, kicked 673 goals and scored 80 tries.

Douglas Clark, a Cumbrian, made his Huddersfield debut in 1909 and went on to play 485 games – a Huddersfield club record for appearances in a career – scoring 99 tries. He won three Challenge Cup winners medals, three League Championship medals and seven Yorkshire Cup winners medals. He gained 31 Cumberland caps and played in 11 Test matches against Australia and New Zealand, touring with the Lions in 1914 and 1920. Clark, who received eighteen shrapnel wounds at Passchendaele during the First World War, was also a champion wrestler.

Huddersfield 1914/15, the sublime 'Team of All Talents'. Following on from Hunslet (1907/8 season), they became the second team to win all four trophies available to them. Only 19 games were lost between 1911 and 1920. *Back row, left to right:* A. Bennett (trainer), A. Lee, J.W. Higson, H. Banks, E. Jones, E. Heyes, F. Longstaff, D. Clark, A. Swinden, H. Bennett (assistant trainer). *Middle row:* R. Habron, M. Holland, S. Moorhouse, H. Wagstaff (capt), T. Gleeson, G. Todd, B. Gronow. *Front row:* Yorkshire League Cup, W.H. Ganley, Northern League Cup, A. Rosenfeld, Northern Challenge Cup, J. Rogers, Yorkshire Challenge Cup.

All Four Cups in Rozzy's, a tobacconist's shop next to the Empire cinema in John William Street. From left to right are T.H. Grey, A. Bennett and Albert Rosenfeld.

Major Holland, a full-back, made his debut in 1909. However, it was not until 1911/12 that he commanded a regular first-team place. A 119–2 scoreline had been registered by the 'Team of All Talents' in a Challenge Cup triumph over Swinton Park on 28 February 1914 in which Major Holland grabbed a club record 18 goals and 39 points. In total he made 218 appearances for the Fartowners (6 tries, 262 goals).

On 8 April 1916, a North of England Military XV played the ANZACs under rugby union rules at Headingley before a crowd of 10,000, with proceeds going to war charities. In the lineout (white jerseys) are Douglas Clark (directly under the ball) and Ben Gronow (seventh from the right). The North won 13–11.

THREE

BETWEEN THE WARS

Huddersfield were back to full strength in 1919/20, winning the Yorkshire Cup, Yorkshire League and NU Challenge Cup, plus they were runners-up in the League Championship Final losing 3–2 to Hull, albeit minus five players who had departed for the 1920 Lions Tour to Australia. From left to right are Ben Gronow, Harold Wagstaff, Johnny Rogers, Gwyn Thomas and Douglas Clark.

Huddersfield 1921/2, Yorkshire League winners. *Back row, left to right:* A. Clayton (trainer), H. Lodge Esq, T. Fenwick, W. Watts, F. Stamper, A.B. Canby Esq, A. Swinden, J. Leeming, D. Clark, B. Gronow, A. Sherwood, J. Clifford Esq, S. Abbey Esq, S. Moorhouse, H. Bennett (assistant trainer). *Front row:* J. Rogers, A. Davidge, S. Williams, G. Thomas (capt), J. May, D. Jessop, H. Wagstaff, J. McTigue.

Team building continued at
Fartown and, on 14 December
1926, Leonard Charles Bowkett,
a centre three-quarter, was
signed from Coventry RU. Under
Bowkett's leadership, Huddersfield
won successive League
Championships in 1928/9 and
1929/30. He also played full-back
for England against Wales in
1932. From 1926 to 1935,
Bowkett made 274 appearances
for Huddersfield, scoring 37 tries
and kicking 305 goals.

Ernie Mills, an Australian wing
three-quarter, joined Huddersfield
in 1927 after the ban on British
clubs signing Australian players
(imposed since 1913) was lifted.
A prolific try-scorer, he stayed
at Fartown until 1935, playing
336 times (290 tries, 23 goals).
He is seen here taking some of
the 1929 Australian tourists for
a drive.

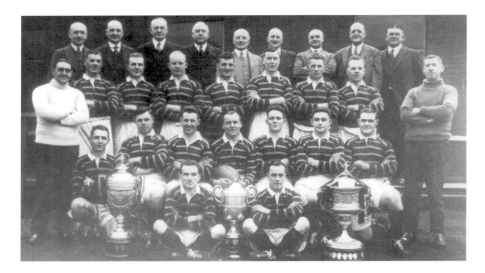

The Huddersfield side of 1928/9, winners of the League Championship, Yorkshire League and the Halifax Infirmary Cup. *Back row, left to right:* H.G. Roebuck, F. Wright, M. Sutcliffe, R. Lockwood, Sir Joseph Turner KBE JP (president), H. Brook, F.B. Hoyle, F.H. Clifford, C.L. Reynard (secretary). *Third row:* J.T. Withers (trainer), J.L. Baxter, C.W. Morton, H. Young, C. Halliday, P.G. Carter, J. Rudd, H. Tiffany, W. Overton (assistant trainer). *Second row:* J. Stocks, J. Brook, E. Mills, L.C. Bowkett (capt), G. Parker, F.G. Smart, S. Gee. *Front row:* E. Williams, S. Spencer.

Halifax 7 Huddersfield 13 at Thrum Hall on 26 December 1929 – the ball in the loose closely watched by Harold Young. Young, who played 121 times for Huddersfield (17 tries), earned his first and only Test cap during the Australians' tour to England in 1929/30, and helped Cumberland win Championships in 1927/8 and 1932/3.

Henry Tiffany signed for Huddersfield in September 1924 and took part in four cup successes – the Challenge Cup victory of 1932/3, the League Championship of 1929/30 and the Yorkshire Cup victories of 1926 and 1931. He made 403 appearances (40 tries, 2 goals) with Huddersfield. In 1950/51 he was Huddersfield's assistant trainer, and after fifteen years in total with the Fartowners, retired at the end of the 1961/2 season.

Huddersfield 1929/30, League Championship, Yorkshire League and Huddersfield Royal Infirmary Cup winners. *Back row, left to right:* S. Gee, T. Banks, J. Rudd, C. Halliday, H. Young, H. Tiffany, C. Morton. *Middle row:* W. Overton (assistant trainer), J. Brook, S. Brogden, J. Stocks, L. Bowkett (capt), E. Mills, G. Parker, F. Smart, J.T. Withers (trainer). *Front row:* E. Williams, Yorkshire League Cup, E. Thompson, Huddersfield Royal Infirmary Cup, S. Spencer, League Championship Cup, F. Royston.

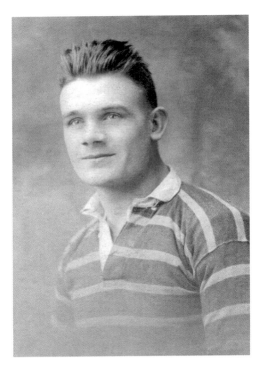

Herbert Sherwood played for Huddersfield from 1927 to 1941, following on from two of his uncles, Clon and Arthur, both whom had lengthy spells at Fartown. Sherwood, who took part in both Wembley finals of 1933 and 1935, played 407 times for Huddersfield (21 tries, 155 goals). He played for two seasons after the outbreak of the Second World War and then joined the navy. He died in Rio de Janeiro, Brazil, while on active service.

Fartown's 1932/3 season had gathered momentum only after three January signings – Ray Markham, the Australian 'flyer'; Fred Brindle, a loose forward from Hull KR and Leslie Adams from Leeds. Markham's impact was significant, going on to make 263 appearances for the Fartowners, scoring 255 tries and 3 goals.

Huddersfield paid their first visit to Wembley in 1933, opponents Warrington also making their debut in the capital. Another first was the royal guest, HRH the Prince of Wales, later to abdicate the throne as Edward VIII. The game was accepted by all contemporary experts as being the best of the pre-war Wembley finals.

Huddersfield's Cup Final squad outside Harrow station (London) on their arrival on the evening of Friday 5 May 1933. From left to right are Banks, Sherwood, Halliday, Markham, Norcliffe, Bowkett, Brindle, Richards, Brogden, Adams, Talbot, Scourfield, Spencer, Tiffany, Mills and Parker.

Huddersfield and Warrington take the field at Wembley, Saturday 6 May 1933. The Fartowners were captained by Len Bowkett (right) while Warrington were led by Bill Shankland. The attendance was 41,874 with receipts of £6,465.

Stan Brogden in action during the 1933 Cup Final. Brogden joined Huddersfield from Bradford Northern on 4 August 1929 for a record-breaking fee of £1,000. He won 16 Great Britain caps, 9 while with Huddersfield, 7 with Leeds, played 4 times for England and gained 19 Yorkshire caps. He played 156 games for Huddersfield (90 tries, 1 goal).

Huddersfield beat Warrington 21–17 in a classic encounter in the 1933 Cup Final. The last Huddersfield try was scored by stand-off Gwyn Richards, pictured at the point of touchdown being tackled by Warrington full-back Billy Holding. On the extreme right is Fartowner Stan Brogden, while Tom Blinkhorn and Bill Shankland of Warrington look for confirmation.

Len Bowkett, who kicked six goals in the final, proudly collects the Challenge Cup from HRH the Prince of Wales, who told him that he had 'enjoyed the match immensely.' Huddersfield had lifted the trophy for a record fourth time in front of a new record crowd for a final.

Huddersfield 1932/3. *Back row, left to right:* C.L. Reynard (secretary), F.B. Hoyle (committee), H. Brook (committee), H.G. Roebuck (vice-chairman), Sir Joseph Turner (president), R. Lockwood (chairman), M. Sutcliffe (committee), F. Wright (committee). *Third row:* C. Brockbank (trainer), H. Tiffany, C. Halliday, F. Brindle, E. Norcliffe, H. Sherwood, F. Talbot, W. Overton (assistant trainer). *Second row:* G. Richards, T. Scourfield, E. Mills, L. Bowkett (capt), R. Markham, S. Brogden, G. Parker. *Front row:* L. Adams, S. Spencer.

Alexander Erskine Fiddes, a Scottish rugby union trialist from Hawick, signed for Huddersfield in October 1933, making his debut against the Australian tourists at Fartown on 18 November 1933. A superb centre, he went on to play 467 games for the Fartowners, scoring 200 tries and kicking 166 goals.

Huddersfield returned to the twin towers of Wembley two years later, 1935 marking the Silver Jubilee of Their Majesties King George V and Queen Mary. The Huddersfield team is introduced to Mr J. Lewthwaite (Chairman of the Rugby Football League) by Milford Sutcliffe (Chairman of Huddersfield). From left to right are Tiffany, Sherwood, Watson, Roberts, Davies, Richards and Scourfield.

Huddersfield defend their try-line in the 1935 final as Castleford press home an attack. The Huddersfield players are, from left to right, Watson, Davies, Talbot, Tiffany, Scourfield and Sherwood. The Fartowners were clear favourites to beat Castleford in the final, but on the day were more easily defeated than the 11–8 scoreline suggests.

Huddersfield 1934/5. *Back row, left to right:* Roberts, Fuller, Talbot, Fiddes (capt), Scourfield, Sherwood, Watson, Mountain. *Front row:* Tiffany, Markham, Mills, Richards, Davies. Markham was the leading try-scorer with 41 in 43 games, while Sherwood kicked 70 goals.

Huddersfield's Welsh contingent in 1935/6 included, from left to right, Tom Scourfield, Stanley Mountain, Dai Evans, Gwyn Richards, Glyn Prosser, Idris Towell, Billy Johnson, and Dennis Madden. Madden played for Aberavon RFC and joined the newly-formed Acton and Willesden RL Club in 1935 where he gained the first of his seven Welsh RL caps. He made his Huddersfield debut against Hull at Fartown on 14 December 1935.

William Harold (Billy) Johnson played rugby union for Newport before signing for Huddersfield in December 1934. A prolific try-scorer for Huddersfield (126 tries in 196 appearances), he won his only Welsh RL Cap against England during January 1938, and in April and May of the same year he toured France with a British Rugby League party.

Huddersfield 1938/9, winners of the Yorkshire Cup. *Back row, left to right:* W.H. Johnson, H. Sherwood, G. Gray, A.E. Fiddes, D. Shaw, D. Evans, E. Hughes. *Front row:* W.J. Taylor, R. Bailey, R.T. Markham, T.L. Grahame, S.V. Pepperell, D. Madden. The last season of peacetime football brought the Fartowners their ninth Yorkshire Cup success.

Huddersfield beat Hull 18–10 in the Yorkshire Cup Final on 22 October 1938, as Odsal staged its first major final before a crowd of 28,714. The Huddersfield and Hull teams line up prior to the final and referee Frank Fairhurst from Wigan holds the ball.

Action from the 1938 Yorkshire Cup Final at Bradford. Hughes (Huddersfield) contests the ball with three Hull players, Ellerington, Booth and Barlow. The other Huddersfield players are, from left to right, Sherwood, Evans, Shaw, Grahame and Bailey.

Alex Fiddes, the captain of Huddersfield, lifts the Yorkshire Cup after defeating Hull. Markham (3) and Madden scored Huddersfield's tries, with Fiddes (2) and Madden adding the goals. Huddersfield players in the picture are, from left to right, Johnson, Evans, Sherwood, Taylor, Madden, Markham and Grahame.

Huddersfield 1939/40, 'Sevens' winners at Odsal and Parkside. *Back row, left to right:* Bailey, Gray, Sherwood, Markham. *Front row:* Johnson, Grahame, Fiddes, Stan Pepperell. Huddersfield, led by Alex Fiddes, adept at the game he learned so well in the Scottish Borders, were acknowledged Sevens champions in pre-war seasons 1936, 1938 and 1939.

Pictured in the old tiled bath at Fartown, shortly before the Second World War are, from left to right, Ron Bailey, W.V.P. Morgan and J. Regan. Ron Bailey, with fellow Australian Tom Grahame, arrived in Huddersfield in December 1937 – the last two to beat another overseas ban imposed by the Rugby League. Bailey (84 appearances, 19 tries) returned home in 1940, playing in Australia and after the war he represented his country.

FOUR

GLORY DAYS:
THE 1940s & '50s

Huddersfield 1944/5, winners of the Challenge Cup. In the last two-legged final of the war years, Huddersfield beat Bradford Northern 7–4 in the first leg at Fartown and 6–5 in the second at Odsal with two guest players in the side. *Back row, left to right:* J. Wood-Beever, F. Wright, W. Cunningham (chairman), H.V. Wood (president), R. Lockwood, F.B. Hoyle, H. Holt (assistant trainer). *Middle row:* C.L. Reynard (secretary), J. Aspinall, L. Baxter, K. Mallinson, W. Leake, G. Brook, A. Givvons, S. Spencer (trainer). *Front row:* J. Burrow, J. McGurk (Swinton), J. Bawden, A.E. Fiddes (capt), T.L. Grahame, A.J. Pepperell, J. Miller (Warrington).

Rugby League Challenge Cup Final, Second Leg, Bradford, 5 May 1945, Huddersfield 13 Bradford 9 (aggregate for the two games). Alex Fiddes holds the Challenge Cup outside the dressing rooms at Odsal. Miller, a guest player from Warrington, enjoys a quick smoke after the game.

Jeff Bawden, from Hensingham ARL, Cumberland, signed professional forms on 23 October 1943. Bawden represented Cumberland on 14 occasions and was unlucky to miss out on the 1946 Lions Tour to Australia. His last game for Huddersfield was against Leigh at Fartown on 20 December 1952. A prolific scorer for the Fartowners, he played in 243 first team games for Huddersfield, kicked 515 goals and scored 91 tries for a total of 1,303 points.

Les Baxter joined Huddersfield from local club Netherton, made his first team debut against Oldham at Fartown in the War League on 4 September 1943, and played until 1949. A solid, dependable back row forward, Baxter appeared for Huddersfield in both legs of the 1945 Challenge Cup Final. He played 123 times for the Fartowners, scoring 14 tries.

The Huddersfield team which drew 10–10 at Batley, 12 January 1946. *Back row, left to right:* Burrow, Albert Pepperell, Nicholson, Bawden, Whitehead, Baxter. *Front row:* Booth, Bradbury, Givvons, Fiddes, Robson, Winkworth, Leake.

The Huddersfield team which finished League Championship runners-up to Wigan are given a civic reception at Huddersfield Town Hall on 18 May 1946. *Back row, left to right:* Taylor, Baxter, J.P. Mallalieu MP, J. Wood-Beever (committee), Morgan, Robson, Mallinson, Anderson. *Front row:* Leake, W.T. Davies, W. Cunningham (committee), Fiddes, Alderman Mary E. Sykes (mayor), Burrow, Russ Pepperell, Bawden.

Jock Anderson was a native of Hawick, Scotland. Anderson stunned the Scottish rugby union scene by becoming a Fartowner on 19 January 1946; his signature was obtained at the end of the Scotland v New Zealand game at Murrayfield. Nicknamed the 'Flying Scotsman', he quickly became popular with Fartown supporters, playing until 1952. He made 114 appearances, scored 74 tries and kicked 21 goals.

Half time in the match at Wakefield, 13 March 1948. The autograph hunters get busy with, from left to left, Des Thomas, Pat Devery, Jeff Bawden (signing), Morgan (about to sign) and Len Howard.

Huddersfield 25 Wigan 5, Fartown, 28 August 1948. A packed terrace looks on as Paddy Reid cuts through to make the first Fartown try scored by Hunter (centre) while Lionel Cooper (right) awaits the outcome. Mountford, Ratcliffe and Blan are the Wigan players.

Huddersfield 1948/9, winners of the League Championship and Yorkshire League. *Back row, left to right:* S. Williams, H. Lockwood, B. Gronow, W. Cunningham, H.V. Wood, J. Wood-Beever, A. Dews, W. Stoker. *Third row:* R. Nicholson, J. Maiden, J. Daly, R. Robson, D. Valentine, J.L. Davies, I. Owens, G.V. Hughes. *Second row:* A. Archbell, G. Wilson, J. Anderson, J. Bawden, P. Devery, L. Cooper, J. Hunter, M. Meek, A. Fiddes. *Front row:* S.V. Pepperell, W. Banks, G.R. Pepperell, A. Ferguson.

Huddersfield players setting off for the League Championship Final at Maine Road, Manchester, on 14 May 1949. From left to right are Valentine, Daly, Maiden, Hunter, Cooper, Pepperell, Anderson, Devery and Nicholson. Inside the coach are Dr Barrett and Hubert Lockwood.

The 1949 League Championship Final between Huddersfield and Warrington attracted a record crowd of 75,194. It was also a cliffhanger finish with the Fartowners winning a close game 13–12. The picture shows Helme (Warrington) trying to elude Cooper and Owens (right).

Pat Devery with the 1949 League Championship trophy. He played for Balmain from 1944 to 1947 and represented Australia (3 times) and New South Wales (6). Huddersfield signed him in September 1947, and in 1952/3 his 16 tries and 142 goals set a club record of 332 points in a season. In all, he made 223 appearances (98 tries, 401 goals) for a total of 1,096 points.

Lionel Cooper represented Australia in all three Tests against the 1946 Great Britain Lions. The man responsible for enticing him and Johnny Hunter to Huddersfield in 1947 was broadcaster Eddie Waring. His 10 tries against Keighley in November 1951 is still a club record for tries in a match. From 1947 to 1955 he played in 333 games, his try aggregate of 420 a long-standing Huddersfield club record for tries in a career. Added to that, he kicked 42 goals for a total of 1,344 points.

Huddersfield won both their matches on their week-long tour of France during November 1949, but only by narrow margins, beating Carcassonne 12–7 and a Catalan XIII 14–12 at Perpignan.

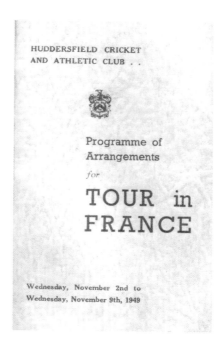

HUDDERSFIELD CRICKET
AND ATHLETIC CLUB . .

Programme of
Arrangements
for

TOUR in FRANCE

Wednesday, November 2nd to
Wednesday, November 9th, 1949

Puig Aubert (left), captain of Carcassonne, presents Jeff Bawden with a pennant before the start of the game during Huddersfield's tour of France in 1949. Aubert was arguably the greatest French rugby league player of all time. Playing for Carcassonne, Les Catalans, Celtic de Paris and Castelnaudary, he won five French championships, four French cups and represented the French national side on 46 occasions.

Huddersfield 1949/50, League
Championship and Yorkshire Cup beaten
finalists, Yorkshire League winners.
Back row, left to right: Cracknell, Bowden,
Owens, Nicholson, Wagstaff, Valentine.
Middle row: Wilmot, Cooper, Devery
(capt), Hunter, Meek. *Front row:* Banks,
G.R. Pepperell.

Johnny Hunter, a full-back from
Eastern Suburbs, Australia, signed for
Huddersfield in 1947 as part of the
double deal with Lionel Cooper. Hunter's
play was hazardous, thrilling and
spectacular, with opponents instructed
'whatever you do don't kick the ball
to Hunter!' He played 333 games for
Huddersfield (62 tries, 3 goals) and
became one of the best full-backs ever to
wear the Claret and Gold.

Huddersfield, winners of the Yorkshire Challenge Cup against Castleford at Leeds on 4 November 1950. *Back row, left to right:* Robson, Wilmot, Bawden, Cracknell, Clark, Owens. *Middle row:* Wagstaff, Bowden, Pepperell, Cooper, Banks, Mundy, Valentine, Tom Matthewman, Nicholson. *Front row:* Alex Fiddes, Hunter.

In a tour match played at Fartown on 1 November 1952 before a crowd of 25,494, Huddersfield lost to Australia 9–27. *Back row, left to right:* Devery, Curran, Large, Griffin, Cooper, Brown, Valentine. *Front row:* Rylance, Slevin, Hunter, Pepperell, Banks, Henderson.

Peter Henderson arrived in Huddersfield from New Zealand on 27 September 1950. He made seven appearances with the All Blacks RU side before turning professional, and represented his country as a sprinter in the Empire Games of 1950. Henderson made two representative Rugby League appearances and played for the Other Nationalities team on five occasions. He played 251 times for Huddersfield, scoring 211 tries.

Huddersfield half-back Billy Banks breaks away from the scrum during the Challenge Cup Semi-Final 7–0 win against Wigan at Odsal on 28 March 1953, witnessed by a crowd of 59,022. Banks, from Maesteg, joined Huddersfield in August 1948 and gave great service to Wales RL, playing in seventeen internationals. He made 281 appearances for Huddersfield (41 tries, 4 goals).

Eighteen years and one world war later, the Fartowners returned to Wembley on 25 April 1953. The previous few finals had been lacking a little 'needle' and had been relatively one-sided affairs. Those who enjoyed keen rivalry would no doubt include the 1953 final between Huddersfield and St Helens near the top of the ranking.

Huddersfield beat St Helens 15–10 and gained their second win at Wembley in three appearances in front of a crowd of 89,588. There were injuries which caused controversy, especially the one sustained by Hunter in an off-the-ball incident, as well as nineteen-year-old Peter Ramsden who had his nose broken.

Mr Wilf Stoker, the Football Committee Chairman, leads Russ Pepperell and the Huddersfield team out at Wembley.

Stand-off Peter Ramsden's second try, the winning score. There were five minutes remaining and the scores locked at 10–10 when Ramsden, a solidly built sound tackler and forceful runner, took a pass from prop Jim Bowden near the half-way line to clinch victory for Huddersfield.

Huddersfield captain, Russ Pepperell, receives the Challenge Cup from His Grace the Duke of Norfolk. The Fartowners, who went through the game with misfortune, pain and loss, emerged as deserved cup winners for the sixth time.

Russ Pepperell holds the cup aloft at Wembley. Also hoisted is Peter Ramsden who became the youngest player to win the Lance Todd Trophy. Ramsden's second Wembley appearance came nine years later in May 1962 against Wakefield Trinity. He played 246 games for Huddersfield (54 tries, 2 goals).

Huddersfield 1952/3, winners of the RL Challenge Cup and Yorkshire Cup. *Back row, left to right:* J.T. Withers, W. Cunningham, H. Lockwood, J. Wood-Beever, H.V. Wood, W. Stoker, B. Gronow, T. Matthewman, A. Archbell. *Third row:* H. Tiffany (assistant trainer), J. Brown, W. Griffin, J. Bowden, J. Large, J. Cooper, E. Slevin, D. Valentine, J. Waring (masseur), W. Smith (trainer). *Second row:* R. Cracknell, P. Henderson, J. Hunter, R. Pepperell (capt), L. Cooper, P. Devery, R. Rylance. *Front row:* W. Banks, RL Challenge Cup, Yorkshire Cup, P. Ramsden. Inset: G. Curran.

Cumbrian Russ Pepperell made his Huddersfield debut in September 1939. An exceptional talent in terms of versatility and undoubted leadership, he played fifteen years for Huddersfield, was captain from 1946 to 1953, making 365 appearances (125 tries, 2 goals). He gained 16 Cumberland caps, played for England 4 times and also captained a British Empire XIII in May 1949.

The five Huddersfield players selected in the Great Britain squad for the inaugural World Cup competition held in France in 1954. From left to right are Dave Valentine, Billy Banks, Mick Sullivan, Ron Rylance and Harry Bradshaw.

Dave Valentine from Hawick was an inspirational member of the post-war Huddersfield side which dominated the late 1940s and early 1950s and will always be remembered for his captaincy of the victorious Great Britain side in the 1954 World Cup. Valentine ended his Huddersfield playing career in November 1957 having made 356 appearances in the Claret and Gold, scoring 72 tries.

When Billy Boston played for Huddersfield! Huddersfield and Hunslet players took part in two testimonial matches for Lionel Cooper, with Billy Boston wearing the Claret and Gold in the Fartown game on 9 May 1955. The players enjoying a pre-match joke are, *clockwise from left*: Bill Griffin, Jack Large, Russ Pepperell, Arthur Clues, Billy Boston, Lionel Cooper.

Hull second row Markham is unable to prevent Huddersfield stand-off Jack Barker scoring a try in a 26–5 win at Fartown on 8 September 1956, as Mick Sullivan (centre) looks on.

Huddersfield 1956/7. *Back row, left to right:* Fairbank, Hunter, Bradshaw, Griffin, Briggs, Valentine. *Front row:* Barker, Henderson, Slevin, Smales, Dyson, Sullivan, Wainwright. Pat Devery retired in 1954, Cooper and Pepperell in 1955, and the 1956/7 season saw the departure of such players as Billy Banks, Johnny Hunter, Bill Griffin and Jim Bowden, shortly to be followed by Peter Henderson, marking the end of a Fartown era.

A familiar landmark at Fartown was the half-time scoreboard, presented to the senior club by the HC & AC Supporters' Club. It was first put in to use on 10 November 1956 when the Australian tourists were playing at Fartown. The Omega clock had been operating since February 1931.

The Huddersfield 'A' team that played Keighley 'A' at Fartown on 26 October 1957. *Back row, left to right:* Iredale, Colburn, Wainwright, Heap, Close, Dixon, Shacklady. *Front row:* Clarke, Aldred, Cecil, Quinn, Brasch, Curry. From 7 December to 12 April they were unbeaten and got into the Top Four of the Yorkshire Senior Competition, losing 8–9 to Hull in the semi-final play-off.

Huddersfield 1957/8. *Back row, left to right:* Plunkett, Wood, Lister, Bowman, Barrow, Sullivan, Briggs. *Front row:* Cecil, Smales, Valentine, Dyson, Slevin, Kilroy. The season proved to be yet another transitional one – Jack Large retired, Peter Henderson returned to New Zealand, Sullivan was transferred to Wigan and Valentine retired after breaking his ankle for the third time. The team, however, proved worthy winners of the Yorkshire Cup.

Action from the Yorkshire Cup Final at Headingley, Leeds, on 19 October 1957, as Huddersfield defeated York 15–8. Brian Briggs breaks through the York defence on a charge to the line. Brian Smith (a future Huddersfield coach) is the wing three-quarter alongside Briggs.

Mick Sullivan signed for Huddersfield from Shaw Cross Boys Club on 29 May 1952. He was quick, direct and decisive and his defence was notoriously hard. His 46 Tests for Great Britain (41 tries) were ample testimony to his durability. Sullivan left Huddersfield for Wigan in 1957 for a world record £9,500 – he had played 117 times, scoring 93 tries.

The Huddersfield team of 1959/60. *Back row, left to right:* Curry, Slevin, Breen, Shacklady, Killen, Close, Flint, Lockwood. *Front row:* Ramsden, Barrow, Ashcroft (capt), Dyson, Smales. Ernie Ashcroft led the team well and missed only one game, with Tommy Smales topping the try-scoring list. Frank Dyson played for Great Britain against Australia and captained Yorkshire.

FIVE

THE 1960s & '70s

Huddersfield 1960/1. The Fartowners were beaten 16–10 in the Yorkshire Cup Final by Wakefield Trinity at Headingley, Leeds, on 29 October 1960 – the last occasion Huddersfield were to appear in a Yorkshire Cup Final. *Back row, left to right:* Devereux, Noble, Thornley, Bowman, Wood, Breen, Brown. *Front row:* Wicks, Gorman, Dyson, Ashcroft, Smales, Slevin.

Tommy Smales races through a gap during Huddersfield's 6–0 Challenge Cup semi-final win against Hull KR at Odsal Stadium, Bradford, on 14 April 1962. Huddersfield progressed to Wembley thanks to three goals from full-back Frank Dyson.

Huddersfield were the surprise package of the season, with Trinity the hot favourites and on course to emulate Huddersfield's 'Team of All Talents' by lifting all four major trophies. Trinity's Neil Fox kicked three drop goals which made up the winning margin of 12–6 after each side scored a brace of tries, Smales and Ramsden getting the Fartown scores.

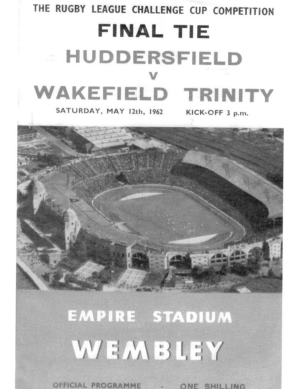

THE RUGBY LEAGUE CHALLENGE CUP COMPETITION

FINAL TIE
HUDDERSFIELD
v
WAKEFIELD TRINITY

SATURDAY, MAY 12th, 1962   KICK-OFF 3 p.m.

EMPIRE STADIUM
WEMBLEY

OFFICIAL PROGRAMME   -   ONE SHILLING

Led by their respective chairmen, Mr Stuart Hadfield and Mr Bill Cunningham, the Huddersfield and Wakefield teams march on to the Wembley turf before the start of the game.

The Huddersfield team is presented to Earl Alexander of Tunis before the match. He is seen shaking hands with Leo Booth who was making his first Challenge Cup appearance of the season. Also seen are, from left to right, Bill Cunningham, Tommy Smales, Ray Haywood, Aidan Breen and Frank Dyson.

Wembley, 1962. Its 'eyes down' for, from left to right, Ken Noble, Tommy Smales, Don Close and Aidan Breen, as they make sure that the Fartowners get possession of a loose ball.

Leo Booth holds on to Trinity's Geoff Oakes during the 1962 Wembley final, with Mick Clark in support. Other Huddersfield players are, from left to right, Tommy Smales, Harry Deighton, Don Close and Aidan Breen.

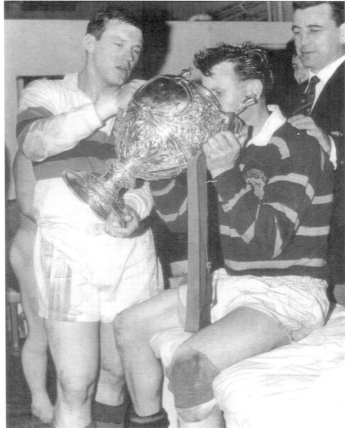

Neil Fox takes the Challenge Cup into Huddersfield's dressing room after Trinity had beaten the Fartowners at Wembley in 1962. Fartown skipper Tommy Smales takes a drink while Huddersfield coach Dave Valentine looks on.

14-5

★ Wakefield full-back Gerry Round finds the odds of five to one too much to overcome

THAT'S HAPPY HUDDERSFIELD

IT'S sweet revenge for Huddersfield. Yesterday at Odsal they beat Wakefield 14—5 to win the Rugby League Championship Cup. Last week they went to Wembley and were beaten 12—6

★ Ouch! That hurts. Huddersfield defenders Peter Ramsden and Austin Kilroy stop Wakefield's Milan Kosanovic with a bone-crushing double tackle.

EDDIE WARING'S REPORT PAGE 30

Now it's Peter Ramsden's turn to be tackled. Wakefield captain Derek Turner brings him down—hard !

A week after the Challenge Cup Final, Huddersfield took revenge in the League Championship Final at Odsal, Bradford, when they defeated Wakefield Trinity 14—5 to deprive them of 'Four Cups' glory. Wicks and Smales scored the tries, Dyson adding four goals.

Tommy Smales, the captain of Huddersfield, shows the Mayor of Huddersfield, Alderman H.F. Brook JP, the League Championship trophy at a civic reception given to the team on their return from Odsal.

Huddersfield, League Champions 1961/2. *Back row, left to right:* H. Lockwood, G. Armitage, W. Cunningham (chairman), E. Sheard (president), T. Matthewman, G. Bottomley, F. Hobson, P. Crabtree. *Third row:* H. Tiffany (assistant trainer), L. Booth, A. Redfearn, D. Devereux, K. Bowman, E. Slevin, F. Dyson, D. Valentine (coach), K. Senior (secretary). *Second row:* G. Davies, A. Breen, M. Wicks, T. Smales (capt), P. Ramsden, H. Deighton, A. Kilroy. *Front row:* R. Haywood, D. Close

Mike Wicks, a wing three-quarter, signed for Huddersfield from Torquay RU in August 1959. A serious neck injury in March 1960 marred his early career. A difficult player to stop, he scored 51 tries and kicked 2 goals for Huddersfield in 80 appearances, before retiring from the game at the end of the 1961/2 season.

Trainer Mel Meek gives a team talk to the players prior to their Eastern Championship Final against Hull KR on 10 November 1962. Huddersfield were hoping to add the Eastern Division trophy to the season's bag; unfortunately they lost 10–13. From left to right are Close, Redfearn, Noble, Bowman, Breen, Kilroy, Lancaster, Smales, Rowe, Ford, Meek and Haywood.

The Eastern Division team that defeated France 23–16 at Carcassonne on 1 November 1962. *Back row, left to right:* Bowman (Huddersfield), Tyson (Hull KR), Fox (Wakefield T), Turner (Wakefield T), Jones (Leeds), Hammill (Featherstone R), Clawson (Featherstone R), Thornett (Leeds). *Front row:* Cowan (Leeds), Paul (Hull KR), Shelton (Hunslet), Flanagan (Hull KR), Smales (Huddersfield).

The Cup Final and League Championship side of the early 1960s was slowly beginning to break up. New faces emerged – one of them was Ken Senior from Moldgreen ARL, seen here on the way to the line at Watersheddings, Oldham, in 1964.

TED SLEVIN

Nowadays it is not unusual to see players of Pacific island origins gracing the rugby league stage. In 1964, however, it was something of a novelty to see Fijians wearing the Claret and Gold of Huddersfield. The four Fijians to arrive at Fartown were, from left, John Ravitale, Tomasi Waqabaca, Josefa Saukuru and Tomasi Naidole.

**HUDDERSFIELD
1951—1962**

Souvenir Brochure
Price 1/-

Consistent, courageous and composed, all those adjectives could be applied to Ted Slevin, Huddersfield's long-serving prop forward. Slevin signed for the Fartowners in October 1951 and played until 1962. In all, he made a total of 441 appearances for Huddersfield (8 tries) – a total bettered only by Douglas Clark, Ken Senior and Alex Fiddes.

The transfer of Tommy Smales to Bradford Northern in November 1964 ended a lengthy association with a player who gave great service to Huddersfield. It was fitting that he should gain the game's highest honours, including captaincy of the Great Britain Test team against Australia in 1963. Smales played 295 times for Huddersfield (111 tries, 1 goal).

Huddersfield 1964/5. *Back row, left to right:* Davies, Slingsby (trainer), Heppleston, Vic Van Bellen, Anderson, Hagan, Valentine, Bowman, Russell, Tomlinson. *Front row:* Calvert, Senior, Curry, Close, Feather, Waqabaca. The team finished in eighteenth position in the league, but did win the Bottom 14 Competition, a 'one-off' event where alternative methods of play-the-ball were experimented with.

Ken Bowman, seen here in action against Wigan, joined Huddersfield from Heworth ARL in April 1955, going on to play 247 times (76 tries) for the Fartowners. He gained three Great Britain caps and also represented Yorkshire. He left to join Bradford Northern in September 1965.

The Huddersfield team that played in a friendly against Halifax at Fartown, 16 August 1965. *Back row, left to right:* Goddard, Heppleston, Dobson, Close, Haywood, Anderson, Ian Van Bellen, Valentine, Longstaff. *Front row:* Hollands, Senior, Curry (capt), Gascoigne, Deighton, Russell. Brian Curry left in the close season to join Oldham. He rejoined Huddersfield in June 1971, and in all played 211 (+ 1 sub) games, kicking 473 goals, 19 tries, for a total of 1,003 points.

Huddersfield, winners of the Sterling Sevens, Fartown, August 1966, beating Castleford 15–6 in the final. *Back row, left to right:* Jimmy Russell, John Anderson, Don Close, Bob Hagan. *Front row:* Rob Valentine, Ken Loxton, Ray Haywood, Paul Longstaff.

Mick Major, Huddersfield's wing three-quarter, scores in the corner against Bradford Northern in the first round of the Yorkshire Cup at Fartown on 3 September 1966, despite the tackle of Alan Rhodes. Major joined Huddersfield from Featherstone Juniors in June 1965 and went on to play 127 games for the Fartowners, scoring 38 tries.

The Huddersfield defence move across to cover Parry Gordon in the game against Warrington at Fartown on 12 November 1966. On the right is Brian Dobson, a mainstay of the pack throughout the 1960s. Dobson signed for Huddersfield from Moldgreen ARL in December 1963 and played 167 (+ 13 sub) games, scoring 12 tries. Other Fartowners are, from left to right, Taylor, Blackett, Loxton, Hagan, Hepworth (on ground) and Valentine.

Fartown: Season 1967/8. Huddersfield coach Harry Street, right, supervises a pre-season training session, led by Mick Major, Paul Longstaff and Albert Bloomfield.

The Fartown floodlights were officially switched on by the president of Huddersfield Cricket & Athletic Club, Mr Robert Hanson, before the game against Hull on 18 October 1967. The match was watched by a crowd of 3,839 – Huddersfield losing 21–13.

An incident from the floodlit game at Fartown against Hull on 18 October 1967. Huddersfield's Booth loses the ball when tackled by Stocks (Hull). Ford (left) and Van Bellen are the other Fartowners in the picture.

In a classic Challenge Cup first round tie at Knowsley Road on 3 February 1968, Huddersfield upset the form book by defeating St Helens 5–0. Here, Ken Senior, Huddersfield's wingman, comes up against Saints great Tom Van Vollenhoven. Alex Kersey-Brown (centre) and Richard Wallace (right) look on.

The touchdown that might have taken Huddersfield to Wembley, but the referee ruled 'no try' for this Rob Valentine effort in the scoreless cup semi-final against Wakefield Trinity at Odsal Stadium on 30 March 1968. Trinity went on to win the replay 15–10 at Headingley the following Wednesday.

Robert Angus Valentine joined Huddersfield in November 1963 and was to become a valuable member of the pack throughout the 1960s. Valentine's form was such that on 9 December 1967, at Station Road, Swinton, he was selected for Great Britain in the Third Test against the touring Australians. He played 164 (+ 4 subs) games for Huddersfield (19 tries, 4 goals).

Graham Naylor feels the force of a Salford tackle in Huddersfield's second round Challenge Cup tie at Fartown on 22 February 1970 – the result, a 0–0 draw. The other Huddersfield players in the picture are, from left to right, Long, Valentine, Taylor, Van Bellen and Close (on ground). Incidentally, Huddersfield lost the replay at Salford 11–4.

On 3 April 1970, Huddersfield reached the semi-final of the Challenge Cup against Leigh at Wigan, again fate taking a hand as the Fartowners were defeated 10–4 in a try-less game. *Back row, left to right:* Irving, Heppleston, Tomlinson, Naylor, Weavill, Davies, Pickup, Leek. *Front row:* Hooson, Wallace, Close, Senior, Bedford, Loxton, Calvert.

Action from the Challenge Cup Semi-Final against Leigh at Wigan, 1970. Frank Davies, who kicked both Huddersfield goals, stretches the Leigh defence, watched by Fartowners, from left to right, Loxton, Leek, Tomlinson, Close, Pickup, Weavill, Senior and Heppleston. Davies was a prolific scorer for Huddersfield, playing in 256 (+ 12 sub) games, kicking 435 goals together with 53 tries since his signing from Normanton ARL in November 1963.

The Huddersfield team that played Keighley at Fartown on 7 October 1972. *Back row, left to right:* Pickup, Weavill, Wild, Veivers, Chawner, Branch, Bennett, Davies, Shepherd. *Front row:* Senior, Hooson, Appleyard, Loxton, Bedford, T. Doyle. The mascot is Michael Kaye. Greg Veivers, on his return to Australia, captained their national side. Wayne Bennett went on to coach Premiership winners Brisbane Broncos, Queensland and Australia.

Huddersfield wingman Dave Hooson, tackled by Bradford Northern's Bernard Watson in a game at Odsal Stadium on 9 April 1973. Hooson, who made 209 (+ 5 sub) appearances (67 tries, 102 goals), signed for Huddersfield from Mixenden ARL on 27 April 1967, was an ideal clubman and one of the most under-rated wingers that Huddersfield ever had.

Ken Loxton signed for Huddersfield from
Normanton ARL on 2 October 1965, and made
213 (+ 4 sub) appearances (4 tries, 2 goals) for
the Fartowners. A superb organiser, he bossed
everything from the acting half-back position.
These attributes helped him attain Great Britain
status, playing in the Third Test of the 1971
series against New Zealand at Leeds.

Huddersfield, Second Division Champions
1974/5. *Back row, left to right:* T. Davies,
Chamberlain, Van Bellen, Heppleston, Branch,
Welsh, Forster, Bedford, Wilson. *Front row:*
Smith (coach), Hartley, Shaw, Hooson, Miller
(capt), Leathley, T. Doyle, Curry (assistant
coach). Insets: Weavill, Knight, Senior. Mascot:
Michael Kaye. Huddersfield nabbed the title
from under the noses of Hull KR, Hartley
kicking 110 goals.

Huddersfield, 1977/8. *Back row, left to right:*
Jeanes, Van Bellen, Leathley, Keean, Branch,
Wroe, Mullany, T. Johnson, Redfearn, Davies,
Morton, Cyrus. *Middle row:* Hutton, Wilson,
Shaw, Senior, Hooson, Clegg, Nelmes, Smith,
Fox, Cramp, Forster. *Front row:* Shepherd,
Schofield, R. Armitage, Ruddock, Greenwood,
Hartley, Leese, Rowe. Neil Fox, the Huddersfield
player/coach, overtook Jim Sullivan's all-time
points scoring record, which had stood since
1946, on 2 January 1978 with the third of
his four goals for Huddersfield in a win over
Oldham. He finished with a career points total
of 6,220 in 828 games, a record unlikely ever
to be beaten.

Ian Van Bellen, who signed for Huddersfield as
a seventeen-year-old from Birkby CYC in June
1963, was a tough, uncompromising 18-stone
ball-playing prop forward, who had two spells
with Huddersfield, comprising 255 (+ 18 sub)
games, scoring 45 tries, 4 goals. His nomadic
career took him to Castleford, Bradford
Northern, Fulham, Blackpool Borough,
Halifax, Kent Invicta and Keighley.

Hugh Armitage (right), Huddersfield's wing three-quarter, on the charge in the game with St Helens at Fartown on 3 September 1978, with, from left to right, Fartowners Tony Johnson, Glenn Knight, Jimmy Johnson and Mick Shepherd awaiting the outcome.

Eighty-two-year-old former Fartown winger Hubert Pogson turns the clock back sixty years as he kicks off the First Division match between Huddersfield and Wakefield Trinity on 29 October 1978, to celebrate 100 years of football at Fartown. Referee Mr J.V. Moss is left of the picture alongside Peter Rowe.

SIX

THE BARREN YEARS
(1980–90)

Ken Senior's illustrious career with Huddersfield came to a close at Doncaster on 23 September 1979, seventeen years after signing from Moldgreen ARL. A Great Britain international and Yorkshire County player, Senior achieved the record number of appearances for a back, second only to Douglas Clark for most appearances in a career for Huddersfield. In 468 (+ 6 sub) games, he scored 212 tries.

Dave Heppleston, who joined Huddersfield from Shaw Cross Boys Club on 6 May 1962, ended his Fartown career at Wigan on 5 April 1981, after playing 348 (+ 26 sub) times, scoring 14 tries and 2 goals. Domestic success came in 1974/5, Heppleston featuring in both prop positions as Huddersfield won the Second Division Championship title.

Huddersfield 9 Wigan 7, 15 March 1981. Six see red at Fartown – Jimmy Johnson, Knight and Lyons from Huddersfield; Hodkinson, Bolton and Kiss from Wigan – after the game degenerated into a free-for-all fight. Huddersfield players pictured are, from left to right, McHugh, Slater, Swale, Punter, Clarke (on ground) and Wood. The referee was Vince Moss.

It took Wigan just 10 minutes to pinpoint Huddersfield's main danger weapon in the game at Fartown on 15 March 1981 – then came a series of high tackles. Tony Johnson, man of the match, was repeatedly being illegally floored before being substituted in the 50th minute. Born in Jamaica, he signed for Huddersfield in July 1973 and played 69 (+ 30 sub) games (11 tries), at one point making the Great Britain U24 squad.

Huddersfield, 1981/2. *Back row, left to right:* J. Johnson, Busfield, McHugh, Cooper, Brierley, Rose, T. Johnson. *Front row:* Mullany, Greenwood, Hetherington, Cramp, Sheard, Leathley. Under coach Les Sheard the club finished in fifth position in a fifteen-team Second Division, with crowds averaging 1,185.

Paul Dixon breaks away from the Batley defence in Huddersfield's game at Mount Pleasant on 29 August 1982, watched by, from left to right, Johnson, Fennell, Hetherington and Walsh.

Ian Hobson, watched by Derek Wroe (left) and Ian Slater (right), takes on the Blackpool Borough defence in a game at Fartown on 6 February 1983, in front of a crowd of 680. The 1982/3 season saw crowds slump to an alarming average of 776, with an attendance of just 422 against Whitehaven on 10 April 1983.

Huddersfield 1983/4. *Back row, left to right:* Wilson, Thomas, Davies Murray, Cramp, Johnson, Fitzpatrick, Rose, Leary (physiotherapist). *Front row:* Punter, Barton, Wroe, Leathley, Blacker, Senior, Bostock. Chairman Roy Brook had been in negotiation with a new consortium who wished to buy HC & AC. On 18 August 1984 new chairman John Bailey, John Hillam and Graham Ramsden joined forces with the existing board as new directors.

Glenn Knight leaves Swinton tacklers trailing for his try in the match at Fartown on 13 November 1983. Knight joined Huddersfield from Castleford in the close season of 1974. He had two spells with Huddersfield (211 + 16 sub appearances, 56 tries, 25 goals + 14 drop), the second one all the more praiseworthy in view of the lean times being experienced by Huddersfield.

A promising break halted by the referee's whistle, as Halifax take on Huddersfield on New Year's Day 1984 at Thrum Hall. Tom Davies makes a break supported by Ian Slater (left), watched by Alan Greenwood (on ground). Davies signed from Sharlston ARL in September 1973 and played 12 seasons for Huddersfield (106 + 49 sub games, 5 tries).

June 1984 – enter 'The Barracudas at Arena 84', a vision of Mr Bailey. The dilapidated state of the Fartown complex can be seen in the disrepair of the George Herbert Hirst Memorial at the entrance to the grounds.

Huddersfield Barracudas 1984/5. *Back row, left to right:* Cramp, Bostock, Leathley, J. Johnson, Rose, George, Murray, Davies, Dixon, Fitzpatrick, Price, Barrett (physiotherapist). *Front row:* P. Johnson, Thomas, Pickerill, Senior, Knight, Hirst, Thornton, Wroe, Blacker. The 1984/5 season was a further year of struggle although average crowds did rise to 905. At the end of the season there were repercussions at every sports ground after the Bradford City fire, none more so than the crumbling Fartown facilities.

Training at Arena 84 in the mid-1980s. From left to right are Brian Blacker (front), David Schofield, Dennis Fitzpatrick, Jimmy Johnson, Peter Cramp, Graham Thornton, Glenn Knight, John Paterson.

Huddersfield's Gary Senior, aided by Billy Platt, foils a Rochdale attack in a first round Challenge Cup tie at Arena 84 on 9 February 1986. In the background are Alan Boothroyd (11) and Phil Johnson (right).

12   Huddersfield Daily Examiner, Friday, April 18, 1986

SPORT

Gripping end to high-scoring draw but

Only 303 people turn up to watch Arena 84 game

By IAN LAYBOURN

Huddersfield Barracudas 32 Keighley 32

A CROWD of just 303—Huddersfield's lowest ever—saw a tremendous fightback and a gripping finish as the sides demonstrated why they have two of the worst defences in the league.

Huddersfield, who have now conceded more than 30 points in each of their last four matches, produced a woeful tackling display in the first half and they looked a well beaten side when they trailed 28-12 after 42 minutes.

But they staged a remarkable comeback, scoring 20 points in 12 bewildering minutes, and suddenly, and quite incredibly, they found themselves 32-28 in front with nine minutes left.

A win that at one stage seemed impossible had become a reality—until the final game took another turn with only a minute Kei...

half chance to cross for an equalising try at the corner.

The match hinged on scrum-half Paul Moses's touchline goalkick but the emergency marksman had already surpassed most people's expectations by landing four goals from five attempts and his last-gasp effort was both low and wide.

The draw was a fair reflection of a game which both sides dominated in turn, usually with scrum possession. Huddersfield were badly beaten for the ball in the first half but the introduction of specialist hooker Billy Cook, immediately after Keighley had taken their 16-point lead, changed things dramatically.

The tricky surface made it awkward for fen rs bu oo m

half, and then they went about the tackle in a half-hearted manner.

The danger signals went up as early as the second minute when second-rower Mick Hawksworth sailed through weak tackling to create a try for stand-off Ricky Winterbottom and full-back Jeff Butterfield and Moses added others inside 26 minutes to make it 16-2, Billy Platt having opened Huddersfield's account with a penalty.

Veteran centre Trevor Leathley marked his 400th senior game by scoring his 107th try after 32 minutes after a blockbusting run from 18st prop Paul Cockerham, but the celebrations were short-lived for slipshod defence enabled Keighley c h Pe Roe t arve o ry er B

Phil Johnson and Leathley resulted in winger Mark Cambell going over for a try just before half-time, and this, with Platt's goal, brought the score back to 22-12.

The visitors, however, appeared to be on their way to a comfortable victory within two minutes of the re-start when Roe touched down after kicking ahead.

It looked all over and the small band of supporters began to vent their understandable anger towards the Huddersfield players and officials.

But perhaps history ought to have forewarned them for, when Keighley last visited Huddersfield—on Boxing Day in 1984—the home side came back from 20-6 down to win 36-20.

It was Cook who sparke off the revival w / forced his v o ol '

Huddersfield's lowest-ever attendance of 303 witnessed an amazing 32–32 draw against Keighley on 17 April 1986. To complete a thoroughly miserable year, the average attendance plummeted to 678, Huddersfield finishing fourth from bottom in the Second Division.

Huddersfield Barracudas, 1986/7. *Back row, left to right:* Chris Forster (coach), Alan Boothroyd, Steve Wills, Mark Campbell, Derek Wroe, Jimmy Johnson, Dennis Fitzpatrick, Simon Kenworthy, Peter Sedgwick. *Front row:* Anthony Farrell, Ian Thomas, Colin Harris, Antony Edwards, Billy Platt, Geoff Munro, Nigel Marshall.

Huddersfield play Workington at Arena 84 on 14 December 1986. Safety regulations following the Valley Parade fire of 1985 threatened to cause the ground to become 'standing room only', both stands being barred to paying spectators. A short reprieve was granted allowing 300 in the main stand until storm damage caused that to be closed for a considerable period.

Peter Cramp made his first team debut against Warrington at Fartown on 28 December 1975. During his eleven years at Huddersfield (206 + 5 sub games, 78 tries, 61 goals) his centre three-quarter partnership with Trevor Leathley was most successful. In a period between April 1979 and August 1981 they only missed playing together twice. His final game for Huddersfield was against Sheffield Eagles on 30 March 1986.

Trevor Leathley made his debut against Castleford at Fartown in a Floodlit Trophy game on 19 September 1973. He was the master of the interception try, setting up tries not just for himself but for his wingman Peter Cramp. Leathley showed a remarkable record of consistency during his thirteen years with Huddersfield (380 + 23 sub games, 110 tries), playing in 169 consecutive games between 11 August 1977 and 11 April 1982. His last game was against Blackpool Borough on 11 May 1986.

Coach Jack Addy with some of the Huddersfield first-teamers in January 1987. From left to right are Simon Kenworthy, Ian Thomas, Paul Cockerham, Antony Edwards, Alan Boothroyd, Dave Nelson and Kevin Brooke. The new Barracudas coach accepted the fact that, with no money to spend, he would have to work with an inherited playing staff. Attendances at Arena 84 slumped to a lowest-ever point with an average of just 524.

Huddersfield, 1988/9. *Back row, left to right:* Mick Blacker (assistant coach), Huck, Diskin, Simpson, Brooke, Kenworthy, Boothroyd, Subritzky, Power, Nigel Stephenson (coach). *Front row:* Cocker, Senior, Thomas, Gibson, Farrell, Lee St Hilaire, Shuttleworth, McIntosh, Phil Johnson ('A' team coach). The 1988/9 season saw John Bailey abandon the universally disliked 'Barracudas' tag, offering to 'give the club away' to anyone who would take on responsibility for rugby and improve the ground to retain a safety certificate. A three-man consortium of Mick Murphy, Jim Collins and Neil Shuttleworth took over in November 1988 and, slowly but surely, the great old club was dragged up from near oblivion.

Anthony Farrell played for
Huddersfield from September
1986 until October 1989
(68 + 7 appearances, 13 tries,
3 goals) representing GB Colts
and GB U21s while with the
club. He joined Sheffield Eagles
in 1989, moving on to Leeds
Rhinos in 1996. 'Faz' played in
the 1998 Grand Final, the 1999
winning Challenge Cup Final
and represented England against
France in 1999. However, he
elected to play for Wales in the
Millennium World Cup. Leaving
Leeds he joined Widnes Vikings
and later went on to coach
Halifax.

In August 1989, an anonymous
Australian burst on to the scene
- his name, Wally Gibson. In
his first game at Whitehaven
on 3 September 1989, Gibson
scored three tries in a 34–22
win. Gibson's cavalier attacking
football from the full-back
position reminded some of the
older supporters of the great
Johnny Hunter – praise indeed.
He played 86 + 1 sub games for
Huddersfield (50 tries, 13 goals
+ 3 drop goals) before leaving to
join Oldham during the 1992/3
season.

Wally Gibson shoots between Paul Lord and John Henderson of Oldham, with Gary Senior supporting, in the Challenge Cup preliminary round at Watersheddings on 14 January 1990.

Huddersfield 1990/1. *Back row, left to right:* McTigue, Tony Chapman, Sewell, Royston, Mountain, Cocker, Simpson, Thomas, Boothroyd, Edwards. *Middle row:* Power, Senior, Huck, Hawkyard, Maskery, Parr, Chris Chapman, Scholes. *Front row:* Mick Blacker (coach), Wilson, Shuttleworth, Dick (capt), Ventola, Cook, Ian Wigglesworth (mascot), Barry Seabourne (team manager). At last the 'dreadful decade' was over. The scoreboard was fully refurbished, with much of the famous terrace-side repaired and seating extended in the main stand. The club had emerged from unbelievable difficulties during the 1980s – the loyal, hardcore support were entitled to more successful times in the 1990s.

SEVEN

THE SLEEPING GIANT AWAKES

Huddersfield went for broke when they appointed the legendary Alex Murphy as team manager in September 1991 providing a catalyst for a boom season.

The Fartowners lost just two matches under the astute management of Murphy and coach Terry Flanagan – at Batley and Barrow – to finish the season four points clear of their nearest rivals to win the Third Division Championship.

Stand-off Jason Gilbert, watched by Greg Shuttleworth, races through a gap in the Keighley Cougars' defence on his way to scoring a try in Huddersfield's 18–14 win at Fartown on 1 March 1992.

Huddersfield players celebrate receiving the Third Division Championship trophy after the game with Hunslet at Fartown on 17 April 1992. From left to right are Chris Parr, Greg Shuttleworth, Gary Coulter, Joe Naidole and Antony Edwards.

Huddersfield 1991/2, first-ever winners of the Third Division Championship. With a remarkable tally of 173 tries, and Simon Kenworthy and Jason Gilbert kicking 70 goals each, the Fartowners ended the campaign just 13 points short of reaching 1,000 in league and cup matches. *Back row, left to right:* Huck, Sewell, Kenworthy, Scholes, Naidole. *Middle row:* Ronnie Burhouse, Karen Hellawell and Sue Ford (physiotherapists), Louise Hamer, Keith Burhouse, Jack Balmforth, Dr David Hooper, Oates, Maskery, Jowett, Boothroyd, Walker, Lomax, Terry Flanagan (coach), Alex Murphy (team manager), David Parr, Les Coulter, Frank Doyle, David Parker. *Front row:* Brian Henley, Mick Murphy, Gilbert, Thomas, Edwards, Gibson, Jim Collins, Chapman, Shuttleworth, Cocker, Senior, Joe Bramley, Neil Whittaker.

The departure from Fartown; the famous old club, its dignity in tatters after decades of neglect and ridicule, had no choice but to move after estimates ranging from £300,000 to £2m would be required to bring the ground up to standard. Fartown's last professional game was on 23 August 1992 against Ryedale-York in a Yorkshire Cup preliminary round tie. Until the new proposed super stadium was ready, ground-sharing with Huddersfield Town AFC at Leeds Road for two seasons became a necessity.

Huddersfield, 1992/3. *Back row, left to right:* Brian Hendy (physio), Rion Pearce, Andy Pucill, Gary Coulter, Jason Fogarty, David Oates, Phil Helliwell, Lee St Hilaire, Terry Flanagan (coach). *Front row:* Jason Laurence, Joe Naidole, Brian Blacker, Neil Flanagan, Gary Senior, Ian Thomas, Chris Chapman, Brad Davies. Huddersfield gained a spin-off from their move when the Rugby League awarded them a warm-up game against Australia who were preparing for the 1992 World Cup Final against Great Britain at Wembley. Predictably, the Kangaroos won 66–2, Huddersfield's biggest-ever home defeat at Leeds Road.

The Huddersfield squad which defeated XIII Catalan 23–22 in Barcelona's magnificent Olympic Stadium in 1993. *Back row, left to right:* Les Coulter, Joe Naidole, Andy Sewell, Gary Coulter, Ken Kerr, Andy Simpson, Steve Barnett, Andy Pucill, Ian Thomas, Jason Laurence, Martin Maders, Mick Murphy. *Front row:* Chris Coop, Neil Flanagan, Brad Davies, Phil Hellewell, Brian Blacker, Gary Senior, Richard Pearson, Lee St Hilaire, Paul Meilham, Dave Needham. The game was unofficially billed as the 'European Cup' and was the climax of the Fartowners' eleven-day mini tour which also included a match against a Roussillon representative side in France.

Sunday 28 August 1994 – Huddersfield play their first-ever game at the Alfred McAlpine Stadium, thrashing the visitors Barrow 50–12 in front of a crowd of 4,300. Flying winger Brimah Kebbie (5) touches down for his try.

Record up in lights – Dave King (left) and Laurent Lucchese reflect on Huddersfield Rugby League Club's record-breaking score, as the team hammered Blackpool Gladiators 142–4 in a first-round Regal Trophy game at the McAlpine Stadium on 26 November 1994.

Greg Austin, a player who could justify the nickname 'try machine', scored nine tries in the 142–4 rout of Blackpool Gladiators on 26 November 1994. All were typical Austin efforts, backing up breaks left, right and centre, finishing in a style that over the years became his trademark. Austin joined Huddersfield from Salford on 18 August 1994 and in just 66 appearances for the Fartowners scored 74 tries and kicked 25 goals (+ 1 drop).

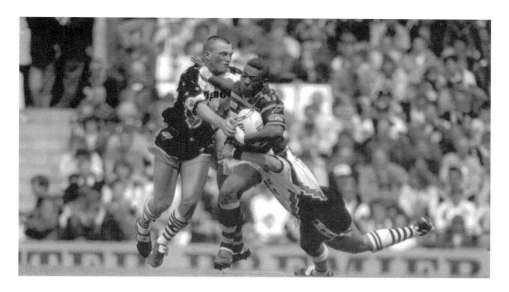

Sunday 21 May 1995, Huddersfield were back where they rightfully belong – on the big stage. The Fartowners appeared at Old Trafford, Manchester, against the Keighley Cougars in the Second Division Premiership Final – the club's first final for thirty-three years. Unfortunately, Keighley were the better team on the day with a 26–6 triumph. Here, Fartown flyer Simon Reynolds is halted by Nick Pinkney and Andy Eyres.

Huddersfield RLFC 1995 Premiership Final Squad. *Back row, left to right:* Phil Hellewell, Roy Ventola, Dean Hanger, Andy Pucill, Richard Pearson, Johnny Bruce, Brimah Kebbie. *Middle row:* Les Coulter (director), Martin Parker (director), Sue Ford (physiotherapist), Karen Hellawell (physiotherapist), Darrell Shelford, Mick Taylor, Garry Coulter, Gary Senior, Martin Maders, Dave King, Basil Richards, Steve Kerry, Alan Bamber (director), Dave Henry (director), Margaret Caldwell (director), Brian Blacker (assistant coach), Barry Smith (director). *Front row:* Mel Green (vice-chairman), Neil Flanagan, Lee St Hilaire, Bob Scott (chairman), Greg Austin, George Fairbairn (coach), Ben Barton, Greg Pearce, Simon Reynolds.

Gary Senior – a consistent performer for Huddersfield at centre or as a tough, no-compromising back row forward. He signed from St Josephs ARL and made his Huddersfield debut from the substitutes' bench against Rochdale Hornets at Fartown on 22 August 1982. Senior played 210 (+ 36 sub) games for Huddersfield in two spells, scoring 57 tries and kicking 21 (+ 1 drop) goals, his last game being the Second Division Premiership Final against Keighley at Old Trafford on 21 May 1995.

Ian Thomas, Huddersfield born and bred, joined the Huddersfield Supporters' Under 17 team more or less straight from school, signing for the Fartowners in May 1983, making his first team debut on 21 August at Barrow in the opening match of the 1983/4 season. Under the coaching guile of Alex Murphy, Huddersfield won the Third Division Championship in 1991/2, Thomas gaining a winners medal. In his twelve-year career with Huddersfield he made 280 + 1 sub appearances, scoring 162 tries and kicking 34 goals.

The first season of summer rugby and the introduction of 'Giants' into the title. Dean Hanger, an Australian and fans' favourite between 1994 and 1998, races in for a try against Salford at the McAlpine on 31 March 1996, encouraged by local product Lee St Hilaire.

Paul Dixon, seen here in action for Great Britain against Australia in the First Test at Wembley in October 1990, signed for Huddersfield from Underbank Rangers ARL in July 1982 – the first of two spells with the Fartowners – leaving in 1985 for Halifax. In a career taking in Halifax, Leeds, Bradford Northern, Sheffield Eagles, Yorkshire and Great Britain, he rejoined Huddersfield in 1997, making 84 + 24 sub appearances in total (32 tries).

Huddersfield Giants 18 Hull Sharks 0 – Divisional Premiership Final, Old Trafford, Manchester, 28 September 1997. Huddersfield scrum-half Ali Davys scores the first try following a kick through from Craig Weston.

The Huddersfield players celebrate their 18–0 victory over Hull Sharks in the Divisional Premiership Final at Old Trafford on 28 September 1997. *Back row, left to right:* Craig Weston, Nick Fozzard, Danny Russell, James Bunyan, Matt Sturm, Dave King, Steve Booth, Andy Cheetham, Joe Berry, Ian Fairhurst (assistant coach), Steve Ferres (coach). *Front row:* Paul Dixon, Basil Richards, Paul Cook, Ali Davys, Tony Bowes, Neil Harmon. On the ground is Phil Veivers.

EIGHT

INTO THE SUPER LEAGUE

When Ken Davy took over as chairman of Huddersfield in January 1996, the club were bottom of the First Division. However, in Davy the Giants had found themselves a real-life knight in shining armour. On Friday 3 April 1998, the dream became reality when the Giants took on reigning champions Bradford Bulls in the Super League III opener at the McAlpine Stadium in front of a crowd of 12,417. Albeit defeated 38–6, Davy declared 'the task for everyone is to move on and make this club the Giants of Super League and Rugby League – the future starts here!'

Huddersfield Giants, 1998. *Back row, left to right:* Harold Box (alliance coach), Danny Arnold, Basil Richards, Tony Bowes, Neil Harmon, Dave King, Jeff Wittenberg, Jamie Field, Paul Loughlin, Trevor Commons (fitness conditioner). *Middle row:* Craig Weston, Chris Orr, Danny Russell, Phil Veivers (assistant coach), Ken Davy (chairman), Garry Schofield (head coach), Paul Cook, Andy Cheetham, Paul Jackson. *Front row:* Joe Berry, Steve Booth, Guy Adams, Matt Sturm, James Bunyan, Ben Barton, Dean Hanger.

Danny Russell outpaces Barry McDermott in the game against Leeds Rhinos at the McAlpine Stadium on 13 September 1998. From left to right, Paul Cook, Mark Moxon and Jamie Field look on. Russell, a hooker signed from Carlisle Border Raiders at the start of the 1997 season, played 83 (+ 15 sub) games for Huddersfield (22 tries). His last game was against Halifax Blue Sox on 17 September 2000.

Legends gather for the opening of Huddersfield RL Club Players' Association Hall of Fame at the McAlpine Stadium on 22 April 1999. An initial twenty-one Fartown greats were chosen, with five of the surviving players attending the ceremony – from left to right are Ken Senior, Peter Ramsden, Tommy Smales, Jeff Bawden and Russ Pepperell.

Paul Reilly in determined mood against Castleford Tigers on 12 September 1999 with Martin Gleeson (left) and Steve Booth (right) in support. A current England international, Gleeson played three seasons for Huddersfield from May 1999 to September 2001 (50 + 9 sub games, 18 tries), moving on to St Helens, then eventually to Warrington Wolves and Wigan Warriors.

Huddersfield-Sheffield Giants. Formed from a merger of former Huddersfield Giants and Sheffield Eagles on 1 October 1999, the newly formed club fared no better than the old Giants, despite the influx of new players who came to it from the Eagles, finishing bottom of the league for the third season in a row. It didn't last long – on 7 September 2000, the club decided to drop 'Sheffield' from the name and revert to being Huddersfield Giants.

Gene Ngamu eyes up a shot at goal in a rare 16–14 win over Wakefield Trinity Wildcats on 3 September 2000. Huddersfield experienced a hard time of it in the early years of Super League and lost 81 out of 99 games between 1998 and 2001, managing to avoid relegation until the end of 2001.

Huddersfield Giants 2001/2, NFP Grand Final Winners, NFP League Winners, Buddies National League Cup Winners. *Back row, left to right:* Meirion Jones (physiotherapist), Turner, Walker, Rice, Reilly, Cruckshank, Hayes, Atkins, Jason Davidson (development officer). *Middle row:* Frank Doyle (kitman), Steve Moslin (masseur), Whittaker, Molyneux, Crabtree, Wittenberg, Roberts, Slicker, Lee St Hilaire (U19s coach). *Front row:* Langley, Cooper, O'Hare, March, Tony Smith (head coach), McNamara, Gene, Moxon, Thorman.

As Tony Smith led the Giants to their unbeaten NFP league campaign of 2001/2, Steve McNamara was a controlling influence throughout, with his superb goal-kicking a significant plus. Signed from Wakefield Trinity Wildcats in September 2000, he played in 78 + 10 sub games, scoring 8 tries and kicking 283 goals, before leaving to join the coaching staff at Bradford Bulls at the end of the 2003 season.

Brandon Costin was the Giants' talisman in his three seasons with Huddersfield – an influential Australian signed from Canberra Raiders in 2001. He joined Bradford Bulls at the end of 2001, winning a World Club Challenge winners medal as the Bulls defeated Newcastle Knights 41–26. He re-signed for Huddersfield in September 2002 and went on to play 73 games in total (46 tries, 97 goals + 3 drop).

Action from the Powergen Challenge Cup Semi-Final against St Helens at the Helliwell Jones Stadium, Warrington, on 25 April 2004. Stanley Gene's run is halted by Paul Sculthorpe (on ground) and Martin Gleeson. Gene, a versatile, fearless performer, topped 100 appearances for Huddersfield, scoring 57 tries.

Galpharm Stadium, 11 March 2005. Huddersfield's full-back Paul Reilly plants the ball over the Widnes line, to the delight of Marcus St Hilaire and dejection of Gary Connolly (left) and Andrew Emilio. After ten years the stadium's naming rights were due for renewal and the McAlpine Stadium became known as the Galpharm Stadium, named after a pharmaceutical concern.

Michael De Vere, Huddersfield's Australian Test centre, seals the Giants' stunning 30–12 Powergen Challenge Cup Semi-Final victory over Leeds Rhinos with his try to add to the five goals he kicked in the match at Odsal Stadium on 30 July 2006. De Vere played two seasons with Huddersfield (2005 and 2006) kicking 101 goals.

Huddersfield Giants line up before the Powergen Challenge Cup Final against St Helens at Twickenham on 26 August 2006. From left to right are Ken Davy (chairman), Jon Sharp (head coach), Thorman, Reilly, Aspinwall, Gannon, Drew, Jackson, Crabtree, De Vere, Paul, Wild, Nero, Donlan and Snitch. Playing in their first Challenge Cup Final for forty-four years, there was to be no fairytale ending – at the final hooter it was 42–12 to the Saints.

Twickenham, 26 August 2006. Australian Brad Drew moves in to tackle Jayson Cayless of St Helens in the Powergen Challenge Cup Final. Drew was at Huddersfield from 2005 to 2007 (82 + 9 sub games, 17 tries, 25 goals + 1 drop) and was the lynchpin in the Giants' side – when he played well the whole team performed. He rejoined Huddersfield for the 2010 season after completing two years at Wakefield Trinity Wildcats.

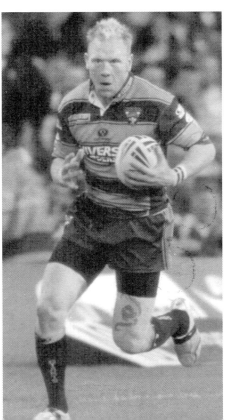

Paul Reilly was eighteen when he signed for his hometown club from Moldgreen ARL in May 1996. An England international, he earned the Jean Galia Medal as man of the match against Ireland in the final of the European Nations Cup in 2004. Fearless at full-back, Reilly gave great service to Huddersfield over eleven seasons, scoring 53 tries in over 200 games.

Australian Chris Nero arrived at Huddersfield Giants from St George Illawarra in October 2003. A dangerous runner out wide, he represented the joint Anzac team that played Cumbria in 2004. Usually a back-rower, he successfully covered in the three-quarters throughout his Giants career (110 + 8 sub games, 48 tries), joining Bradford Bulls for the 2008 season.

Stephen Wild joined Huddersfield Giants from Wigan Warriors in September 2005. A Great Britain, England and Lancashire Origin representative, he was the first-ever Huddersfield player to be selected for the Super League Dream Team (pictured) at the end of 2007, as well as being the first Huddersfield player since Ken Loxton in 1971 to win GB honours. From left to right are Fozzard (St Helens), Demetriou (Wakefield Trinity Wildcats), Mogg (Catalans Dragons), Wellens (St Helens), Roby (St Helens), Burrow (Leeds Rhinos), Peacock (Leeds Rhinos), Penny (Warrington Wolves), Donald (Leeds Rhinos), Ellis (Leeds Rhinos), Barrett (Wigan Warriors), Morrison (Bradford Bulls) and Wild (Huddersfield Giants).

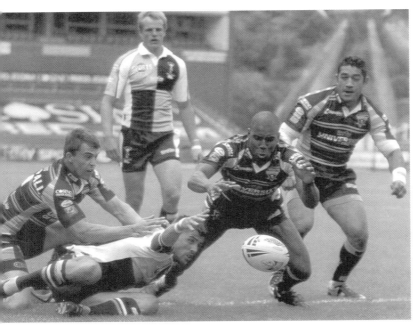

Michael Lawrence, flanked by Martin Aspinwall (left) and Jamahl Lolesi (right), scores a try against Harlequins RL on 22 June 2008. Rated one of the best young prospects to come out of Huddersfield for some time, Lawrence toured Australia with the England Academy Under 18 squad during 2008.

Headingley, 27 August 2008. Rod Jensen proudly hoists the trophy after Huddersfield Giants became the first winners of the Carnegie Floodlit Nines, storming to a 20–4 final triumph over Hull FC. The victorious Giants squad was Thorman, Cudjoe, Jensen, Lawrence, Crabtree, Robinson, Wild, Raleigh, Kirmond, McGillvray, Jones, Barber, Lopag, Lyons and Johnson.

Strong-running prop Eorl Crabtree is currently the longest-serving player at Huddersfield, making his debut against London Broncos from the substitutes bench on 13 April 2001, and to date has made more Super League appearances for Huddersfield Giants (165) than any other player. He represented England against Russia, France and Ireland (final) in the European Nations Championship in 2004, and in friendlies against France and New Zealand in 2005. Crabtree played for England against France in Paris on 13 June 2009 and was included in Tony Smith's England squad for the 2009 Four Nations series against Australia, New Zealand and France.

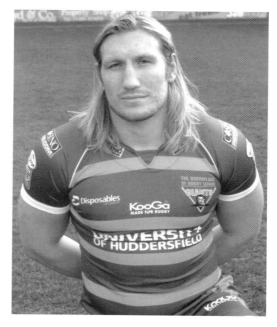

Huddersfield hooker Scott Moore gets the ball away as he is tackled by former Giants player Stuart Jones in the 16–14 win over Castleford Tigers in the sixth round Challenge Cup tie at the Galpharm Stadium on 31 May 2009. Moore, on a season-long loan from St Helens, played for England against France in Paris on 13 June, was named in the 2009 Super League Dream Team and included in the England squad for the 2009 Four Nations series.

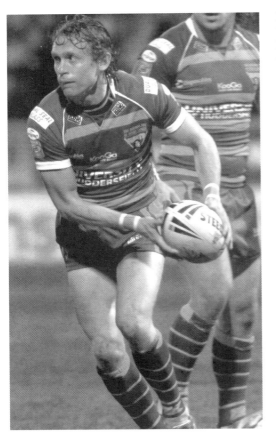

Brett Hodgson, a slightly-built full-back from Wests Tigers, had a tremendous first season with Huddersfield in 2009 (15 tries, 98 goals). He was voted by his peers as Super League Man of Steel, won the Rugby League Writers' Association player of the season and was selected in the 2009 Super League Dream Team, a 'double' success having been named in the NRL's version – the Dally M awards, named in honour of former Australian rugby league great Herbert Henry 'Dally' Messenger – when he was voted full-back of the year in 2005, a season in which he topped the NRL scorers charts with 308 points.

Huddersfield Giants Chairman Ken Davy (left) and Head Coach Nathan Brown lead out the team at Wembley in the Carnegie Challenge Cup Final against Warrington Wolves on 29 August 2009. Brown, who arrived at the Galpharm from St George Illawarra in November 2008, also guided Huddersfield to third place in Super League XIV and into the end-of-season play-offs, earning him the accolade of engage Super League Coach of the Year.